W9-ANC-239

WITHDRAWN

WITHDRAWN

JIMMIE JOHNSON

IN THE FAST LANE

David and Patricia Armentrout

Rourke
Publishing LLC
Vero Beach, Florida 32964

© 2007 Rourke Publishing LLC

All rights reserved. No part of this book may be reproduced or utilized in any form or by any means, electronic or mechanical including photocopying, recording, or by any information storage and retrieval system without permission in writing from the publisher.

www.rourkepublishing.com

PHOTO CREDITS: All photos ©Getty Images

Title page: *Pit crews race to get their drivers back on the track.*

Editor: Robert Stengard-Olliges

Cover design by Nicola Stratford

Library of Congress Cataloging-in-Publication Data

Armentrout, David, 1962-
  Jimmie Johnson / David and Patricia Armentrout.
     p. cm. -- (In the fast lane)
  Includes index.
  ISBN 1-60044-217-X
  1. Johnson, Jimmie, 1975- 2. Stock car drivers--United States--Biography.
3. NASCAR (Association) I. Armentrout, Patricia, 1960- II. Title. III.
Series.
  GV1032.J54A76 2007
  796.72092--dc22
  [B]
                                    2006010978

Printed in the USA

CG/CG

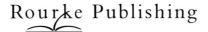
Rourke Publishing

www.rourkepublishing.com – sales@rourkepublishing.com
Post Office Box 3328, Vero Beach, FL 32964
1-800-394-7055

TABLE OF CONTENTS

JIMMIE JOHNSON

Jimmie Johnson has a job most people can only dream about. He earns big money driving racecars. Jimmie is one of the hottest young stars in **stock car** racing's most prestigious series, **NASCAR**'s Nextel Cup.

Born: September 17, 1975
Organization: NASCAR
Car: Chevrolet #48
Car owner: Jeff Gordon
Team: Hendrick Motorsports
Sponsor: Lowes

Young NASCAR fans patiently wait for Jimmie's autograph.

WINNING ON TWO WHEELS

Growing up in California, Jimmie spent most weekends traveling with his family from one race to the next. Racing was a way of life for the Johnson family.

Jimmie began his own racing career at a very young age. In fact, he won his first **championship** when he was only eight years old, and he did it on two wheels. That's because Jimmie got his start racing motorcycles.

Jimmie's family encouraged
his love of racing.

A RACING CAREER

Jimmie switched to four-wheel racing when he was just a teenager. He spent several years racing off-road buggies and trucks throughout the Southwest.

Jimmie's success in the off-road circuit drew the attention of many in the racing world. He met important people who helped jump-start his career. With the assistance of his new contacts and old friends, Jimmie was offered a shot driving stock cars in American Speed Association (ASA) races.

Jimmie learned long ago that racing is all about the fans. Here, he celebrates a victory by raising a cloud of smoke.

A PASSION FOR STOCK CARS

Stock car racing was always Jimmie's true passion, and as usual he wasted no time rising to the top. Just as he had done in off-road racing, Jimmie quickly became a top line competitor, impressing nearly everyone who saw him race. After finishing fourth in the ASA point standings, Jimmie was named the 1998 ASA **Rookie** of the Year.

Jimmie also started three races in NASCAR's Busch series in 1998. The Busch series is one step below the Nextel Cup (formerly Winston Cup).

Stock car racing is a dream come true for Jimmie.

ROAD TO THE TOP

Jimmie continued racing full time in the ASA series in 1999, finishing third in the point standings, one notch above his 1998 season finish. He also added five Busch starts to his growing list of accomplishments.

In 2000, Jimmie ran in the Busch series full time. In 31 starts he finished in the top-ten six times. He ended the year tenth in the point standings, but more importantly, he was gaining the experience he needed.

Racing in NASCAR's Busch Series helped Jimmie gain valuable experience.

The year 2001 was a big year for Jimmie. He recorded his first Busch series victory at Chicagoland Speedway. He also posted nine top-ten finishes. He ended the season eighth in the point standings.

Having honed his driving skills in the ASA and NASCAR's Busch series, Jimmie was ready for his next challenge.

NASCAR'S CUP SERIES

With only a few years of experience racing stock cars, Jimmie was ready for NASCAR's Winston Cup series. His 2002 rookie year would surprise nearly everyone, except maybe Jimmie himself.

Jimmie started 36 Winston Cup races in 2002. He won three races and finished in the top-ten 21 times. Not bad for the new kid on the block. Jimmie came in second in the points race for the Rookie of the Year award, just behind Ryan Newman.

Jimmie finished fifth at the 2001 Busch series NAPA Auto Parts 300 in Daytona.

FAST FACTS

NASCAR Point System for Each Race

Winner	driver earns 180 points
Runner-up	driver earns 170 points
3rd-6th position	points drop in 5-point increments (3rd position-165 points, 4th-160, 5th-155, and 6th-150 points)
7th-11th position	points drop in 4-point increments
12th-42nd position	points drop in 3-point increments
Last place	driver earns 34 points

**Drivers can earn bonus points for leading
a lap and leading the most laps**

*Pole-sitter Jimmie Johnson
drives next to #12 Ryan
Newman at the Pocono 500.*

A WINNING TEAM

Jimmie finished fifth in the Winston Cup point standings in 2002, just seven points behind Jeff Gordon, one of NASCAR's most dominant drivers. Jimmie and Jeff couldn't be happier with the results. The two are teammates. Both drive for Hendrick Motorsports. In addition, Jeff is the owner of Jimmie's car. Make no mistake, both drivers are extremely competitive and are in it to win, but they don't mind rooting each other on.

FAST FACTS

A special point system is used to determine the Rookie of the Year. Drivers are eligible if they have not run more than seven races in a previous season. Drivers must also compete in at least eight of the first 20 races in their rookie year. The driver with the most rookie points at the end of the season wins the award.

Jeff Gordon congratulates Jimmie after his 2002 NAPA Auto Parts 500 win.

In 2003, Jimmie had something to prove. He wanted to show that his rookie year was not a fluke. He did not disappoint his fans. He finished second and even surpassed teammate Jeff Gordon who came in fourth.

DRIVER OF THE FUTURE

The year 2004 was huge for Jimmie. He took the **checkered flag** an amazing eight times and recorded 20 top-five finishes. But somehow the championship eluded him. Once again, he finished in second place, a mere eight points behind Kurt Busch and just ahead of; you guessed it, Jeff Gordon.

Jimmie is nothing if not consistent. He completed 2005 fifth in the point standings—four years, four top-five finishes!

Jimmie has proven he can win big races, too. He notched a victory at the 2006 Daytona 500, thrilling his fans for years to come.

FAST FACTS

Nextel replaced Winston as the sponsor for NASCAR's Cup series beginning in 2004.

Jimmie and wife Chandra celebrate a victory.

Career Highlights

2006: Won the Daytona 500
2005: Finished fifth in points
2004: Won eight races. Posted 20 top five finishes. Finished second in points.
2003: Finished second in Winston Cup series points
2002: Finished fifth in Winston Cup series points
2002: Runner-up for Winston Cup Rookie of the Year
2001: Won first Bush series race at Chicagoland Speedway
2000: Raced in 36 Busch series races and finished tenth in the point standings
1998: ASA Rookie of the Year

GLOSSARY

championship (CHAM pee uhn ship) — each driver is awarded points in a race, with winners earning the most. The driver with the most points at the end of a season wins the championship

checkered flag (CHEK erd flag) — a black and white checked banner waved by a race official. The first driver to receive the flag wins the race.

NASCAR — National Association for Stock Car Auto Racing: the governing body for the Nextel Cup, Craftsman Truck, and Busch series, among others

rookie (ROOK ee) a first-year driver

stock car (STOK KAR) — a commercially available car that has been modified for racing

INDEX

FURTHER READING

Burt, William. *Nascar's Best: Stock Car Racing's Top Drivers.*
   Motorbooks International, 2004.
Lemasters Jr., Ron. *Jimmie Johnson: A Desert Rat's Race To NASCAR Stardom.*
   Motorbooks International, 2004.
Cothren, Larry. *NASCAR's Next Generation.* Crestline, 2003.

WEBSITES TO VISIT

www.nascar.com
www.lowesracing.com
www.hendrickmotorsports.com

ABOUT THE AUTHORS

David and Patricia Armentrout have written many nonfiction books for young readers. They have had several books published for primary school reading. The Armentrouts live in Cincinnati, Ohio, with their two children.